Unreasonable Expectations

Jeff Taylor

Phyllis Arnett

ISBN-10: 1723357855
ISBN-13: 978-1723357855

ACKNOWLEDGEMENTS

Writing a book requires a lot of proofing, editing, and rewriting. An important part of the process is to ask the question, "Does this say what I think it says?" It's really hard to know the answer if you are the person who wrote it. So, it is crucial to have someone else's eyes—another brain. Unfortunately, a co-writer is not the person to do that task. The practice of outlining and planning together makes two brains like one.

We were fortunate enough to have some wonderful people to help us. Without them, our labors would not have been as effective.

Our dear friend Judy, English wiz and grammar nerd, read through the manuscript and gave us invaluable editing suggestions.

Phyllis' aunt Gretchen and her daughter Brandi took the time to read it and give us great feedback.

Jeff's sister Sheryl took on the daunting task of reading, questioning, and correcting the manuscript. And then she sat down with us to walk through the marked up pages. Her work made our efforts so much better.

Finally, we want to acknowledge all of the people who lent their stories and examples, named and unnamed, to this book.

CONTENTS

HOW TO USE THIS BOOK

As authors, we have provided the reader with multiple ways to utilize this book. Whether reading on your own, using it as a workbook, or working through it with another person you're going to approach it differently.

There are three activities at the end of each chapter which will help to process all the information. Answer questions to dig deeper; journal your experiences that may have come to mind; and/or sketch a picture to express yourself. Choose one or all.

REFLECT ON THIS

1. What expectations have you decided are unrealistic?

_____
_____
_____
_____

2. Describe your experience with someone whose behavior defined their true nature.

_____
_____
_____
_____
_____

3. Who do you trust enough to talk to on issues or concerns about bullying, control, manipulation or abuse?

_____
_____
_____
_____

REFLECT ON THIS:
ANSWER THE QUESTIONS, EITHER ON YOUR OWN OR AS A COUPLE, AND THEN DISCUSS.

JOURNAL THIS

_____
_____
_____
_____
_____
_____
_____
_____
_____
_____
_____
_____
_____
_____
_____
_____
_____
_____
_____
_____
_____

JOURNAL THIS:
DIG A LITTLE DEEPER AND WRITE OUT YOUR THOUGHTS AND FEELINGS.

PICTURE THIS

PICTURE THIS:
DRAW OR DOODLE YOUR IMPRESSIONS.

INTRODUCTION

What you hold in your hand is a white hot steel rod, forged in the fires of grief, loss, and disappointment. It is a book on relationships and expectations—a book on healthy connections. But it is also a treatise derived from mistakes, failures, and second chances. It is a dissertation on one of the most common oversights in any and all relationships—unmet expectations.

Our second chances gave us the opportunity to practice, test, and prove these principles. This white hot rod has been tempered to set its strength and durability. But, done properly, it will bend without breaking. Even the strongest steel has pliability to make it useful for endurance.

The title may have you confused. We are not advocating unreasonable expectations. Instead we are exposing them. Most of us live with unmet, albeit unreasonable, expectations—with our jobs, friends, children, and, worst of all, with our life partner, the most important person in our lives.

When we start a job, we want to know what is expected of us. We wouldn't think of accepting a position without knowing the job description. It's standard practice. And, knowing and accepting the published job description would seem to be the secret to job success. However, we all know some job situations don't end well. There are often unwritten, unspoken expectations we cannot possibly meet.

When we start a personal relationship, unfortunately there is no standard, no job description to print out. Do we know what's expected of each other? We may think we do. At first. Then, reality sets in. And, if a job can go haywire *with* a job description, how much worse can a personal relationship become without similar guidelines? Do we know and communicate what expectations we have of the other person? And who decides what is reasonable?

Jeff was told by a counselor years ago that he had no right to any expectation that had not been thoroughly discussed and mutually agreed upon. There it is:

Expectations that live only in our heads have no place in the real world until they are identified, voiced, discussed, and agreed upon by all parties that they are reasonable and achievable. All other expectations are unreasonable, and probably unmet.

As the authors, we begin with a recommendation, a disclaimer, and a warning.

Recommendation: To be successful with the methods contained in this book, it is vitally important to know *how* to communicate respectfully, as well as *when* to talk about things; to understand unconditional love and unconditional respect; and to recognize how to fight fairly.

Most of the stuff we've learned, we either learned from reading others' writings or from massive personal failure. Reading a couple of books first will help. It will be more difficult to achieve the goals contained here without having the tools these books will give you.

- *Fighting for Your Marriage* by Howard J. Markman, Scot M. Stanley, Susan L. Blumberg
  OR
- *A Lasting Promise* by Daniel Trathen, Savanna

McCain, and Scott Stanley (Same information as above title for Christian couples.)

- *Love and Respect* by Dr. Emerson Eggerichs
- *How to Stop the Pain* by Dr. James Richards

Also, although it is not the focus here, perhaps the most destructive, unmet expectations come from within. What are the expectations we have of ourselves that are unmet, unreasonable, and unfulfilled that leave us feeling frustrated or discontented? For more on this subject, we refer you to the book: *Expectation Hangover* by Christine Hassler.

Are you still here? Okay. We'll assume that you have acquired the tools to implement these principles.

Disclaimer: We are not experts. Neither of us is a psychologist or a trained counselor, though, Phyllis is a certified life coach, and Jeff spent many years in counseling.

So why should you listen to us? If you choose to, we think you will find honesty without judgment and a plan for enduring for the long haul. These are words of experience. And you know what that means; we learned it the hard way. (The examples used are real stories of real people, whose names have been changed to protect the guilty.) So, if you're not afraid to learn from our mistakes, maybe you can avoid some of your own.

Warning: If you are in a marriage or a long-term committed relationship and you are reading this on your own, just put it down and walk away. This "white-hot rod" will first poke you in the eye, and then alternately may make you want to poke someone else. Please don't be guilty of using self-discovery from this book as a weapon. That is the antithesis of the point.

Finally, we hope this book will either start you on or continue you on a path of regular relationship maintenance. If you change the oil in your car every 5,000 miles, or if you bought a gym membership you actually use, then you will easily understand that it is imperative that you give the same kind of consistent care and attention to your relationships that you give to your car and your body.

We hope you will use this book as a tool to shape, improve, or maintain healthy relationships in your life.

Jeff & Phyllis

EXPECTATIONS

We humans are a mixture of many things: physical, emotional, psychological, social, and spiritual. And all of that gets thrown into the mix when it comes to relationships. Add to that the distinction between desires and needs. Desires are things we want. Needs are what we have to have.

Many years ago, the psychologist Abraham Maslow tried to prioritize those motivations in his theory known as Maslow's Hierarchy of Needs. (Google it.) His work examined healthy people and the stimuli that drive those who progress through these different levels in their lives, eventually achieving some element of transcendence.

But needs, as well as desires, are not the same thing as expectations. At least they shouldn't be. And we must learn to distinguish among them if we want to have healthy relationships. Other writings may cover needs and desires. Here, not so much.

According to the dictionary definition, an *expectation* is the belief about or a mental picture of the future. Further, expectation is anticipating with confidence of fulfillment. We will return to this thought later, but, as you may have experienced or deduced, some expectations are more reasonable and more realistic than others. What we must first understand is that we have them.

So, where do expectations come from? Are they innate (from Nature or coded into our DNA)? Did we learn them from our parents (Nurture)? What about siblings and friends (peer pressure)?

Growing up, Jeff was encouraged, by example, with a strong desire for excellence. Both of his parents excelled in their jobs and in their hobbies. His mom could type 120 words per minute with few or no mistakes. His dad was a trim carpenter that none of his peers or bosses could keep up with. Jeff learned a strong work ethic and a passion for excellence from the way they conducted themselves.

Besides their occupations, his parents' real passion, the one they had in common, was Gospel music. They worked their respective jobs to fund their lives, but lived for the weekends when they could use their talents. His mom was one of the finest Gospel pianists in Oklahoma and surrounding states. His father had an incredible voice and a huge vocal range.

It's no wonder that Jeff told a boss recently, "I'm not motivated by money as much as I am by a desire to be the best at whatever I do." It could be argued that his parents' modeled excellence instilled such an expectation in Jeff.

Phyllis has a different story. Her parents divorced when she was 14 years old. She observed that her mother didn't know how to balance a check book (back when people did that sort of thing). So she decided to enroll in a consumer business class in high school so that she would never be entirely dependent on another person.

Through these and other similar (unscientific) anecdotal evidences and personal experiences, we have come to believe that expectations may come from anywhere. How much of our expectations come from nature or nurture? Who knows? So, we will not spend a lot of time exploring their origins.

> "Most relationship issues come from unmet expectations."

What we care about most in our context is, whatever our expectations and whatever their sources, how do they affect our lives and our relationships? Whether our expectations come from innate origins, modeled behavior, peer pressure, or personal choice, we must come to an understanding that we have them. This requires a strong sense of self-awareness (the subject of our next chapter).

As mentioned in the Introduction, we now turn to the types of expectations that ultimately affect our sense of well-being as well as our most important relationships. What expectations are realistic or unrealistic, met or unmet, reasonable or unreasonable?

Jeff recently stumbled upon an article on marriage that disputed the old-school idea that most problems in marriage stem from the subjects of communication, sex, and money. Instead, the writer insisted, these are only symptoms, and most relationship issues come from unmet expectations.

If you do an internet search of the term "unmet expectations," you will be overwhelmed with the volume of information and opinions out there. Unfortunately, you will be underwhelmed by the lack

"Expectations must be achievable and cannot violate the nature of the individual."

of data that can help avoid them. The conclusion, however, is that this is a real problem in marriages, friendships, parenting, and careers. Unmet expectations can pile up one on top of the another until bitterness and resentment take over.

Expectations are not *met* primarily because of one thing. They are *unreasonable*.

Expectations, whether they are expectations we have for ourselves or others, can be unreasonable for several reasons. They can be unreasonable because 1) we are unaware of them, (2) they are unspoken, (3) they are not mutually agreed upon, or (4) they are unrealistic.

First, awareness of our own expectations requires at least a degree of self-awareness. If we are not aware that we have them, and cannot identify them, we are destined to be frustrated or even bitter.

Second, to be reasonable, expectations must be named and expressed. Although this is only one step in the process, it is a necessary step. And sometimes it is the hardest.

> "Expectations that live only in our heads have no place in the real world."

Third, it is not reasonable to have an expectation of another, unless they have mutually agreed to it. Whether a spouse, a friend, an employee, or even a child, mutual agreement is crucial.

And fourth, expectations must be achievable and cannot violate the nature of the individual. Achievability can be dependent upon the skills and abilities of the individual. It is unwise to ever expect any person to act in a manner other than who they are.

In the next chapter, we begin the process of breaking down the above list, beginning with self-awareness.

REFLECT ON THIS

1. What expectations do you have which may have come from early experiences?

_____

_____

_____

_____

_____

_____

2. List some of your unmet expectations.

_____

_____

_____

_____

_____

_____

3. Which relationships in your life are affected by these unmet expectations?

_____

_____

_____

_____

JOURNAL THIS

PICTURE THIS

SELF AWARENESS

When Betty was six years old, she received a new watch and a bottle of perfume for Christmas. Before the guests arrived for the Christmas dinner, Betty's mother told her, "Now, it's not polite to show off your gifts unless you're asked." When all the guests arrived, Betty tried to be patient and wait for someone to ask about her gifts. She was eager for everyone to see what she had received, but Betty also wanted to be obedient. No one seemed to notice. So, she announced, "If anyone hears anything or smells anything, it's me!"

Little Betty gives us a look into the early development of self awareness. She was aware she wanted her gifts to be noticed. She was unaware of the effect her words would have. Betty was probably startled by the eruption of laughter from the adults. In

17

its maturity, self awareness helps us evaluate the effect our words and actions have on others.

Self awareness is an honest look at who we think we are and who others think we are. It is an objective appraisal and understanding of how we are perceived by those we love and those who love us—a conscious knowledge of our strengths and weaknesses, thoughts, beliefs, and emotions. The benefit of self awareness is the ability to realistically assess our own values, qualities, skills, and behaviors which we can use to cultivate healthy relationships.

> "Self awareness helps us evaluate the effect our words and actions have on others."

The knowledge that self awareness gives us, allows us to understand we have expectations.

The way someone orders a meal at a restaurant, for example, can reveal a lot about the person. Some people take a lot of time to decide, going over and over the menu until they finally settle on the Southwest salad. When they are served, they wish they had ordered what their friend is having.

Someone else may request water without ice, hold the cucumbers on the salad, steak medium rare. They know what they want and how to ask for it. Is one more self-aware than the other? Maybe. Self awareness is a process. We learn to objectively analyze what makes us tick through personal observation and our interactions with others.

> "The knowledge that self awareness gives us, allows us to understand we have expectations."

By contrast, Suzanne doesn't consider how she or anyone else ticks—the why for what they do or how they act. She accepts them at face value, never questioning the reasons. She and her husband would always bicker. She didn't like it, but that's the way he was so that's how it was going to be, never considering it could be different.

Phyllis is starkly self-aware. She starts each day early

in the morning. She is aware she needs enough time in the morning to get fully awake and she enjoys the early quiet-time: no talking, no television, just coffee and a book, crochet, or some other quiet activity.

> "Self awareness should not be confused with self-indulgence."

When her children were still living at home, she made sure to start her day well before anyone else even thought of getting out of bed. Otherwise, she knew she would not be mentally prepared for the day ahead. Not that it always worked. There were some nights spent staying up too late or some mornings one of her children would wake too early. The missed quiet-time resulted in one grumpy mommy. But this just solidified her awareness of the necessity to allow herself that extra hour each morning.

Even now, her children grown and on their own, Phyllis still takes advantage of the early morning hours to begin her day. It is not merely a habit, but part of her *self*.

Obviously, there are different degrees of self awareness. What about the person who is not self-aware? The guy who thinks he can sing, but can't. He is not self-aware. He's not objective. He has an unreasonable expectation of himself perhaps passed on to him by parents, peers, or even teachers. People who have no self awareness may just be self-delusional. To say one is not self-aware is to say they are incapable of stepping back and looking at themselves with reasonable objectivity.

There are people who may not be delusional, but simply don't care and don't see the importance of being self-aware. They may have conscious insight, but exclaim, "This is how I am. Deal with it."

Marian and Carly have planned a coffee date for Thursday at 10:00 a.m. Marian arrives by 9:55 on that day and receives a text from Carly saying she is just leaving the house. It will take her twenty minutes to make the drive to the coffee shop. Carly may be fully aware that she has a tendency to be perpetually late and simply not care. But she may be unaware of the effect her behavior has on those who are always waiting. We'll refer back to this example several times in other chapters. Self awareness should not be confused with self-indulgence.

Aaron and Ashley's relationship suffered from Aaron's refusal to be held accountable for his behavior. They had spent part of their honeymoon at a water park and Aaron's eyes not only wandered, but followed any and all busty bikini-clad women. When Ashley protested, Aaron denied any wrongdoing and suggested her allegations were solely based on her low self-esteem.

Years later, they were having dinner at an Italian restaurant. An amply endowed woman was seated at a nearby booth with her husband. Aaron would not stop staring at her, to the point that the woman asked to switch places with her husband so that Aaron could only stare at her back. When Ashley told Aaron of her embarrassment (for herself and the other woman), Aaron continued to suggest Ashley had a problem with self-esteem. He simply refused to take any responsibility for his behavior.

The Carlys and Aarons in our lives may have a modicum of self awareness, but they don't consider how their self-indulgence and lack of responsibility affect their relationships.

In contrast, the ability to acknowledge our flaws and misbehavior, coming into any relationship, liberates us from self-doubt, self-criticism, and the fear of judgment. We are aware we're not perfect. We are free to be ourselves. We are more accepting of others because we know they are just as flawed.

If we accept the person for who they are and we can live with it, great. Live with it. However, most of the time our relationships are going to be, at the very least, something we must work at, learning how to relate to this person who is different from us. In healthy relationships, we are able to discuss thoughts, feelings, and behaviors with confidence, knowing our motives are centered on a mutual agreement—the betterment of the relationship.

Self awareness is also having the ability to see ourselves through others' eyes and the ability to acknowledge we are not perfect. This liberates us from the "Me versus Them" mentality and transforms our thinking into "Me versus Me." Instead of believing, "Why do they always do this to me?" We begin to ask ourselves, "What can I do differently?"

Robert and Nina were invited to a quesadilla party with several other couples, all of whom were to bring miscellaneous food items. Nina suggested they bring queso dip and, because of their hectic schedules, asked Robert to pick it up at a local Mexican restaurant. "You'll probably want to go after the lunch rush, though," she offered.

Robert replied, "Do you micro manage this way at work?"

At first, Nina was irritated by his remark. *I was just thinking out loud,* she thought. *I was trying to be helpful. I don't need to hear that! But... Do I really try to micro manage people?*

As she allowed her irritation to subside and consider Robert's question, Nina began asking herself other questions: *What are my motives? Where does this come from? How does it make people feel?*

Nina concluded it was an issue of trust, going back to her childhood, growing up with an alcoholic father, and searching for ways to maintain a certain amount of control in her life. Nina realized that by asking Robert to go to the restaurant and instructing him as to *when* he should go, amounted to implying he didn't have the sense to know the lunch-hour would not be the best time. If he had chosen to go during the rush, that decision and its consequences would be his own.

Acknowledging her true motives, Nina was able to understand her need to control, how to release it, and allow others to accept responsibility for their actions.

Ben is a night owl, but Pamela is in bed by 10:00 each night. Ben felt guilty about Pamela going to bed alone, so he would go to bed when she did. He tossed and turned until finally sleeping, only to awaken feeling unrested.

Early in their relationship, Pamela had voiced her preferred night time schedule, yet, Ben had not been aware of the effect going to bed earlier would have on his quality of sleep. He shared his insights with Pamela, explaining he just didn't rest well when he would retire too early. Through this experience, Ben was made aware of his need to retire later.

We can see from the last two examples that self awareness can spring from without or from within. And it's not enough just to be aware, but to communicate with each other our discoveries and insights along the way.

In addition to learning self awareness through our interactions, there are resources and methods that can help us become more self-aware. For example, we can take tests that reveal our personality type and how it contrasts and/or relates to other types. We can discover our "love languages" (*The 5 Love Languages*, by Dr. Gary Chapman). We can be proactive. Ask a trusted friend, for instance, how we are perceived by others.

Finally, equipped with self awareness we learn to acknowledge that personal growth is our own responsibility. If we are not seeking personal growth and seeking more awareness of who we are and how we respond to others, all relationships in our lives will suffer.

REFLECT ON THIS

1. What words or phrases describe you? What makes you tick?

_____

_____

_____

_____

_____

_____

_____

2. How do those closest to you describe you?

_____

_____

_____

_____

_____

_____

3. What tools have you used to become more self-aware?

_____

_____

_____

_____

_____

JOURNAL THIS

PICTURE THIS

IDENTIFY

"You're on your way now? Okay, see you in a bit." Aubrey ended the call and frantically went to the kitchen to prepare dinner for her parents. She opened the pantry and found all the cans were missing their labels. Her son had decided to use them for an art project.

Consider how frustrating the above experience might be. Until we identify expectations, they are as useless as unlabeled cans. It doesn't matter how self-aware a person is; our expectations can only be met if they've been identified.

Remember the person who has trouble ordering a

meal? They are unable to identify what they want and then are unsatisfied with what they get. Similarly, we are unsatisfied in our relationships when we are unable to identify our expectations. Even if we are highly self-aware, it is not enough. We must be able to identify these expectations and understand how our perceived needs influence them.

> "We are unsatisfied in our relationships when we are unable to identify our expectations."

Phyllis knows she has a need to be understood. This need influences her expectations in her relationship with Jeff. She expects him to attentively listen to her. When he does, it gives her a sense of love, security, and respect. If this expectation was not identified, the quality of their communication would suffer.

Similarly, Matt has the sense of accomplishment in providing for his family and expects to earn an adequate income to do so. But if his employer cuts his wages, Matt must decide whether or not his current position is the right one for him. His need to provide steers his expectation and directs his career path. But not all needs translate into expectations.

Our expectations should never be used as an excuse for inappropriate behavior. We may have a personal need for acceptance, control, and independence. But if our expectation is to have these needs fulfilled at any cost, it will cost us dearly.

> "Our expectations should never be used as an excuse for inappropriate behavior."

Sara tells her parents Rob and Milly she wants a new dress for Prom. Rob and Milly discuss and agree on a budget for the dress. Milly and Sara go shopping and spend three times the agreed amount.

Does Milly have an expectation that there will not be consequences for her actions? She may think "I can do what I want," and meet her personal "need" for acceptance, control, and independence. However, violating the agreement produces distrust and is counter-productive. A wall of resentment is built between her and Rob.

On the other side, Rob clearly identified and stated his expectation: their mutually established budget for the dress and Milly's respect for their agreement. Does Milly's "need" for control justify inappropriate behavior?

Some expectations may have been identified by our upbringing. Remember the Golden Rule? "Do unto others as you would have them do unto you." Unfortunately, not everyone lives by it.

Naturally, we think others will behave in a manner we would. But that is almost never true. Assuming people will behave the same way we would is an unreasonable expectation. We think, *I would never do that.*

Take Marian and Carly's relationship, for example. They have agreed to meet each other for coffee at a specific time. Marian would not want Carly waiting on her, so she makes sure she is on time. However, Carly is late to practically every appointment. In fact, she boasts to others about always being late. Marian will most likely always be early or on time. Carly violates the agreed expectation, and her behavior builds a lack of trust in the heart of Marian.

The friendship is strained unless, in cases like this one, the Golden Rule is altered: *Expect people to be themselves.* If they continually prove themselves late, they will always be late because they will always be themselves. That doesn't mean we reject them because their habits are different than our own. We can accept our relationships with others when we expect them to be themselves. This is reasonable. Otherwise, we will always be disappointed.

We experience disappointments in all our relationships. Everyone has been disappointed. But when this happens, it's important to ask ourselves why we're disappointed. Most of the time, if we're being honest, we will conclude there was an unmet expectation. Now, is this expectation some new revelation or is it something we've always known about ourselves and expected of others?

There are some serious conversations we should have with ourselves about what we want, need and expect. What are the deal-breakers? Are these valid needs or merely wishful thinking? How did these expectations form? Are they a deep personal need from within us or have we picked them up from parents, friends, co-workers... society?

This is how it has always been and so I expect it.

But just because Mom had dinner ready every night when Dad got home from work doesn't necessarily mean it's going to happen for us. Regardless of whether it's Mom or Dad or both coming home from work, dinner may or may not be ready.

> "We get to share these expectations with our significant other, spouse, children, parents, friends, bosses, and co-workers."

The point is to label those cans. Identify expectations. Sure, they may be out of date, but they can be recycled, upcycled, downcyled—whatever is necessary to make our relationships better.

Oh, but the fun doesn't stop with a conversation

with ourselves. That's just the beginning. We get to share these expectations with our significant other, spouse, children, parents, friends, bosses, and co-workers. Slowly, over the course of these relationships, we will have multiple opportunities for disappointments... er... *discussions*. The next two chapters cover discussing and, if necessary, even *gasp* compromising on these expectations.

REFLECT ON THIS

1. What expectations of yours or others have caused conflicts in your relationships?

_____

_____

_____

_____

_____

_____

_____

2. If the "Golden Rule" isn't the rule of your life, what is?

_____

_____

_____

_____

_____

3. What expectations are potential "deal-breakers" for you?

_____

_____

_____

_____

_____

_____

JOURNAL THIS

PICTURE THIS

ACKNOWLEDGE & DISCUSS

Once we understand that we all have expectations, once we are able to identify them in ourselves and in those with whom we are associated, and once we speak aloud those expectations, then we must acknowledge and thoroughly discuss them.

One of the easiest ways to mess up a relationship is to assume the other person knows what we want. Expecting someone to know what we want just because we're in a relationship is just plain stupid. Even the most intelligent and intuitive people are not mind-readers.

Early on in the butterfly and rainbows stage of a romantic relationship, a common mistake is to assume this divine being can read our minds. But soon reality sets in. His Queen of Hearts has a tilted crown. Her

Knight in Shining Armor falls from the great heights—off that giant white horse—where she has placed him.

Worse, we assume they would naturally agree to meet these expectations, and we are ready to dish out punishment when they don't. *Off with their heads!*

In our delusions, we think this person who loves us so much and knows us so well should be able to read our minds. We're not always unreasonable, but it is unreasonable to expect someone to know what we want if we never tell them. Ideally, voicing our expectations is a form of respect and trust. We're saying, " I respect our relationship and trust you enough to discuss my expectations."

This can be one of the more difficult steps in the process. A person who likes to "go along to get along" might have a tendency to want to stop at identifying. Especially if they think, *It's no big deal; I can handle that without further discussion.* They may feel they understand the expectation, and they can meet it. And that might be true. For a while.

This is a stereotype, but let's talk about the man who expects his house to be clean, the dishes to be clean, his wife to be clean, and dinner to be on the table at 6:00

every night when he gets home. That may be reasonable and achievable for the first year or two. But then children come along. Or the money gets tight, and they both have to work outside the home. Now it is imperative that the expectation be addressed, discussed, and definitely adjusted.

While the dinner-on-the-table example may be a throwback, smaller instances may end up being just as intense. On the job or in the home, expectations need to be discussed regarding their reasonableness and their achievability.

It's important to state here that *when* we choose to talk it out is about as important as choosing *to* talk about it. Others have written more eloquently about the "when." (See *A Lasting Promise*, by Drs. Trathen, McCain, and Stanley.)

Here are some *never* examples: at bedtime, when they first walk in the door, or during a disagreement. Most of us know this list. We should always pick a time when things are peaceful, choose words wisely, be kind. Here's a great phrase to use to get started: "Is this a good time?"

Regardless, we must not stop at the identify-and-say-it-out-loud stage. We have to talk it out. No matter how difficult, no matter how long it takes. This is the place where the real work gets done. Take those formerly mentioned, unlabeled cans out of the cabinet and open them up. Pry them open together, as a team. Examine the contents. Talk about what's inside, and decide what to do with it.

Jim was an inside salesman for most of his career. In fact, he was the top salesman every year. He had better numbers than the outside sales people. In his industry, his counter was a hangout, because, over the years, clients came to trust him, count on him, and return to him for advice or even to shoot the bull. Whether calling him on the phone or dropping by to swap stories, they knew he would be there Monday through Friday from 8:00 a.m. to 5:00

"In any relationship, expectations need to be thoroughly acknowledged and discussed."

p.m. They knew he had the answer they were looking for, and they knew he had their best interest in mind. They counted on it.

One day, a change in ownership and management brought about the announcement that there were no longer going to be inside and outside sales people. Everyone was going to do both inside and outside selling. Jim was going to be expected to be outside of the building and generating leads and sales at least half of the work week. What should Jim do?

He can try to adjust, change his schedule, change his pattern. He can warn his customer base of his new schedule. Then, he can do what's been mandated to do. Or he can walk into his boss' office and say, "We need to talk about this."

In either case, Jim should request a meeting with the new management to do what we have been advocating: acknowledge and discuss.

In Jim's case, the manager will either leave him alone and let him do what he does best, or not. If not, Jim has a decision to make.

In any relationship, expectations need to be thoroughly acknowledged and discussed.

As we mentioned earlier, Phyllis has a need to be understood. That translates into an expectation that she and Jeff will do what it takes to be certain that Jeff understands her. No matter what they are talking about. It can be feelings or desires or resolving a misunderstanding.

However, that process became much easier once they discussed that expectation. Jeff learned how important it was to her for him to respond. And to respond with more than a grunt or an "Uh-huh," but to acknowledge and to restate what he understands. What a great joy for him to hear her say she feels she has been heard and understood.

Phyllis and her daughter Brandi have a 10-year tradition of watching a movie together, in the theater, on Christmas day. One year, Phyllis was trying desperately to include extended family in the tradition and finding it impossible to accommodate everyone on Christmas day.

Finally, after much discussion, Brandi said, "Can I be honest?"

Phyllis replied, "Of course!"

"What does someone not being able to make it have

to do with our tradition?"

Phyllis was trying to find a day and time to include everyone. Brandi wanted to continue their tradition, but didn't want to make a stink. In the end, their honest discussion led to the meeting of an important expectation: that the tradition continue.

A common pattern of behavior might be to acquiesce. If Brandi had kept silent and gone along with her mom's desire to accommodate everyone else, the tradition might have been interrupted. It's vital that expectations be discussed.

At this point, some might say, "That seems like a lot of work." It is, but only at first. Once it becomes a habit, it is so natural and ultimately so rewarding.

Now, we need to take these examples and apply them to our conversations about any and all expectations. Whether on the job; with a spouse; or with our parents, siblings, and children. Discuss them thoroughly. Listen. Hear and be heard. State and restate. Decide together what is realistic, reasonable, and achievable.

REFLECT ON THIS

1. What expectations have you withheld or acquiesced?

_____

_____

_____

_____

_____

_____

2. Write about a situation in which the expectation of mind-reading caused conflict.

_____

_____

_____

_____

_____

_____

3. What should be the ground rules for open discussions?

_____

_____

_____

_____

_____

_____

JOURNAL THIS

PICTURE THIS

AGREE & COMPROMISE

Working through the progression, we come to the last step. With rare exceptions, this will complete the process.

At this point, voicing our expectations gives us an option: "This is my expectation. Do you agree to it?" When the expectation seems reasonable and achievable, we can agree to fulfill that expectation.

Now, with our mutual agreement, we've completed the process. Unless....

Brenn and Marci were accustomed to their work schedules. Brenn worked days and a few hours on the weekends, while Marci's schedule was more sporadic.

After six years, Marci started a new schedule working four 10-hour days. Marci felt too mentally and physically exhausted to plan, prep, and cook dinner after returning home from a long work day. She asked Brenn if he would take over that task when she had to work late. Brenn agreed.

Marci expected Brenn would, at the very least, have something in mind for their dinner. But again and again she would get home from a long day and need to come up with something on her own.

> "Resist the conclusion that trial and error is the equivalent of trial and failure."

Weeks, months, then a year had passed and Brenn had yet to uphold his end of the agreement. Marci felt frustrated and resentful that Brenn had agreed to take on this responsibility but had not followed through. Finally, she voiced her frustrations.

Sometimes, after an agreement is made, there may be a trial period. What we may have expected would work out easily, may need some adjustments. There's no sense in letting things go on and on before acknowledging it isn't working. We must resist the conclusion that trial and error is the equivalent of trial and failure. *This is a test. It is only a test.*

When the agreement is obviously not working, it's important to revisit the issue, and only when both parties are in a neutral zone. We should never try to have a discussion on the subject (any subject) when one or both people are frustrated and upset. It's important that re-examining an issue not begin with accusations or blame.

We can begin by stating the facts: "This is what we agreed, and it is not happening. What about it isn't working for you?" This is not about confronting someone with what they aren't doing. In a healthy, trusting relationship, it's about considering the possibility there are some wrinkles to iron out in the initial plan.

Brenn and Marci discussed the terms of the agreement again and Brenn confided his insecurities. Marci was such a good cook and foodie, Brenn felt intimidated by making a decision on dinner. He wanted to be helpful, but feared failure. It was easier for him to leave it for her than risk a botched meal.

They decided on a compromise: Marci would plan

the meal, and the two of them would do all the prep together the evening before. This revised expectation was a compromise they could both live with.

Once the steps are followed and discussion has ended, there are three possibilities: (1) We agree the expectation is reasonable and achievable; (2) The expectation as stated may need some compromise; or (3) An expectation which cannot be agreed upon and no compromise can be made is now unreasonable and is either a deal-breaker or no longer an expectation.

REFLECT ON THIS

1. List some of your unmet expectations.

_____

_____

_____

_____

_____

_____

_____

2. Which relationships in your life are affected by these unmet expectations?

_____

_____

_____

_____

_____

_____

3. What is your expectation if a compromise cannot be made?

_____

_____

_____

_____

JOURNAL THIS

PICTURE THIS

UNREALISTIC EXPECTATIONS

To summarize and reflect, expectations will usually go unmet if they have not been identified, spoken aloud, acknowledged and thoroughly discussed, then mutually agreed upon.

However, sometimes expectations go unmet because they are not realistic.

A special note to the reader:

It is unrealistic to expect people with a mental illness or a personality disorder to meet our expectations. Let us hasten to say, there are a lot of wonderful people who are conquering their problems with counseling and medication. But if you are banging your head against a wall because you have followed the right steps and still have unmet expectations, look honestly at each other and ask, "Do either of us have control, manipulation, or delusion issues?" And if the other person looks fine, then maybe it's you. On the other hand, people who think they're crazy usually aren't.

So, we want to encourage you. If you are the victim of a bully, a controller, a manipulator, or an abuser, or if you are the victim of intentional or unintentional gas-lighting, get professional help. Those matters are beyond our scope here. And they will not go away.

> "People who think they're crazy usually aren't."

Beyond mental health issues, there are other reasons for unrealistic expectations. For example, it is not realistic that a 5' 2" 140 pound man can be a lineman for the Chicago Bears. When there are physical and/or talent limitations that prevent one from performing the task, regardless of the desire, the expectation is unrealistic. It is outside the realm of possibility.

Most of us have seen a contestant in a talent show who is not lacking in desire or confidence. However, they lack the ability. Sometimes it is so bad, we are embarrassed for them. Perhaps an overenthusiastic parent convinced them of their dubious capabilities. But it is painfully obvious to us that, for them, becoming a star is simply not in the stars.

Before smart phones and GPS, as a teenager, driving downtown for the first time, Michael called his mother when he found himself lost. As soon as she answered, Michael asked, "Where am I?"

Mom replied, "Now, how am I supposed to know that? What can you see around you? What street signs can you see?"

Michael was so frustrated that his mother could not divine his location that he ended the call.

One thing that we all need to be constantly reminded of, no matter how long we have worked with, lived with, or parented another person, we cannot read someone's mind. We may finish each others' sentences. We may often say the same words out loud, at the same time. But as soon as we decide we can read their mind, we are *both* in for trouble. And, in the same way, we cannot expect other people to read our minds

These examples are all so simple, but nonetheless common. Lack of size, ability, self-awareness, or mind-reading capabilities can make our expectations unrealistic.

Sometimes, even after we have gone through the process we are advocating, there are other reasons that expectations can be unrealistic.

Remember Brenn and Marci's conversation about planning dinner? They discussed it. Brenn agreed to do it. Now, it's an expectation. A reasonable one, right?

> "People cannot and will not be different from who they are."

It never happened. After a year of disappointment for Marci, they talked about it again and reworked the whole idea. Although Brenn was capable and decisive in many other respects, this area was not his strong suit. He did not feel adequate to make this decision for them. It seemed that it violated his nature.

We have all had those people in our lives who have promised one thing and then done another. Some people, like Carly, are perpetually late. Some people, like Milly, have spending problems. Some people have addictive personalities. We can save ourselves a lot of heartache when we realize that people cannot and will not be different from who they are.

In his book *How to Stop the Pain*, Dr. Jim Richards teaches a principle. We can summarize it like this, "When I expect people to be themselves, I am never disappointed." His point, and ours, is that people will always be who they are. No matter what they promise. To expect otherwise is unrealistic and unreasonable.

.

REFLECT ON THIS

1. What expectations have you decided are unrealistic?

_____

_____

_____

_____

_____

2. Describe your experience with someone whose behavior defined their true nature.

_____

_____

_____

_____

_____

_____

3. Who do you trust enough to talk to on issues or concerns about bullying, control, manipulation or abuse?

_____

_____

_____

_____

_____

JOURNAL THIS

_____

_____

_____

_____

_____

_____

_____

_____

_____

_____

_____

_____

_____

_____

_____

_____

_____

_____

_____

_____

_____

_____

_____

_____

PICTURE THIS

CONCLUSION

So many times in our experiences, we think, "What's wrong with me?" Or, "Why can't we just get along?" Our hope is that you found a handful of answers to those questions in these pages.

The steel rod referred to in the Introduction has not been intended as a tool too hot to handle. We have tested, tried, and proven these principles work. It is our hope that you take what we have learned from failure and second chances and use it as a device for molding, shaping, and assisting in your relationships. We believe that these principles and this process will ultimately prove to be helpful, not only in your relationships, but also for your peace of mind.

ABOUT THE AUTHORS

Jeff Taylor and Phyllis Arnett developed a writing partnership during the editing process of Phyllis' children's book *The Ladybug & The Bumblebee.* While working together, they discovered their stylistic compatibility, a similarity of perspective, a common love for writing, and a mutual passion for creative outlet. Their first venture was writing song lyrics together, and, having experienced collaborative success, the logical next step was a book.

Made in the USA
Middletown, DE
22 July 2022

69894121R00046